THE NATURE KIDS GUIDE TO
HUMMINGBIRDS

DAVID ANDERSON

LP Media Inc. Publishing
Text copyright © 2026 by LP Media Inc.
All rights reserved.

For information address LP Media Inc. Publishing,
30012 Variolite St NW, Princeton MN 55371
www.lpmedia.org

Publication Data

Hummingbirds
The Nature Kid's Guide to Hummingbirds — First edition.

Summary: "Learn all about Hummingbirds, the Nature Kid Way"
— Provided by publisher.

ISBN: 979-8-89818-099-7

[1. Hummingbirds – Non-Fiction] I. Title.

Title: The Nature Kid's Guide to Hummingbirds

CONTENTS

HOVERING HOMES

Hummingbirds are important pollinators — they carry pollen from flower to flower as they feed, helping plants reproduce!

Buzz! A tiny bird hovers near a red flower. Its wings move so fast they blur.

Hummingbirds are among the smallest birds in the world. Some are no bigger than your thumb! These amazing birds are among the most acrobatic fliers on Earth.

Hummingbirds live in many places. Some live in warm tropical forests. Others live in cool mountain meadows.

Hummingbirds drink sweet nectar from flowers. They use their long, thin beaks to reach inside blooms. Their tongues can lick nectar up to 13 times per second. These busy birds must eat every 10 to 15 minutes to stay alive.

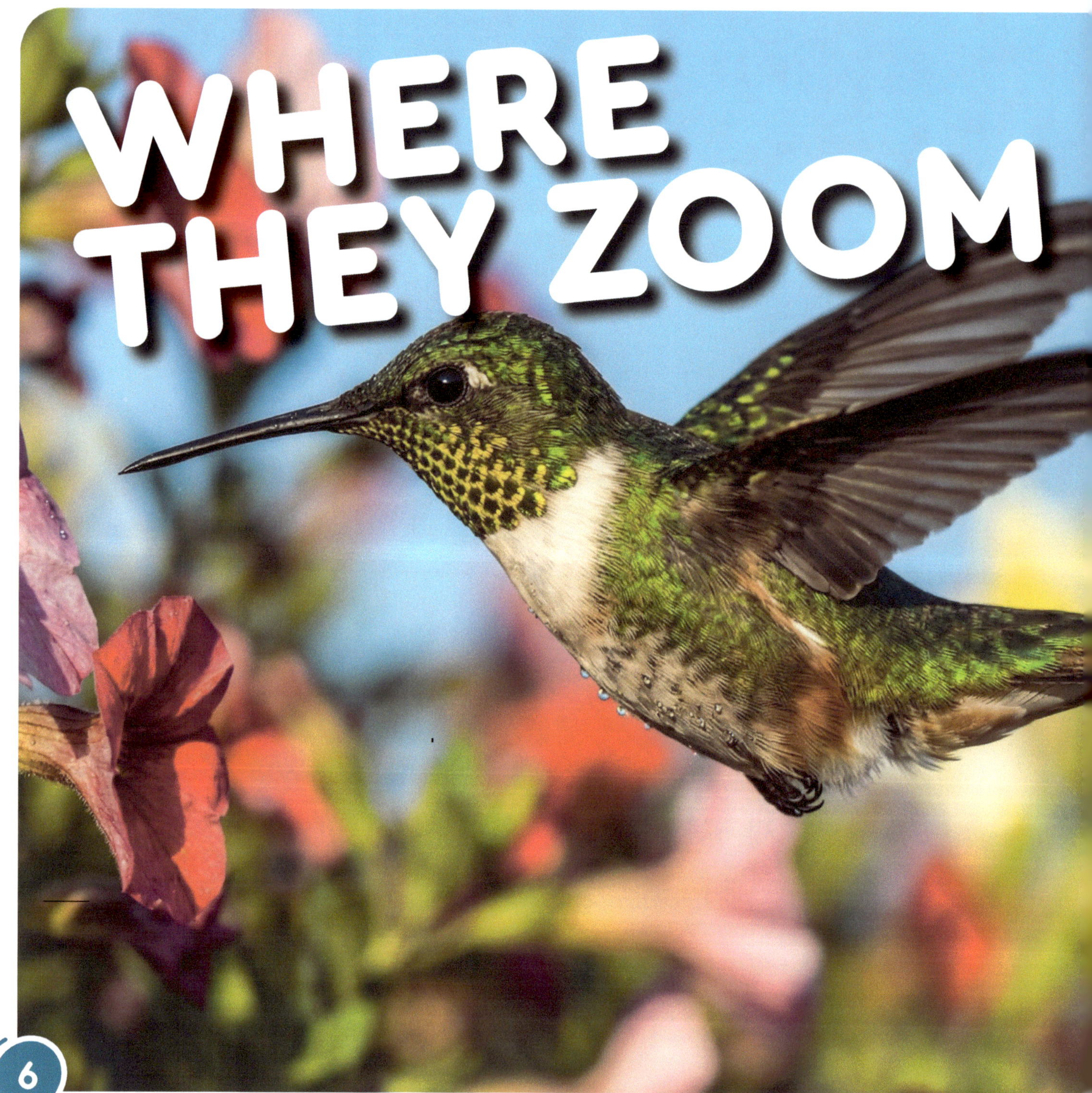

WHERE
THEY ZOOM

Whoosh! A green hummingbird zips through a garden.

Hummingbirds live only in North and South America. You can find them from Alaska to Chile. No other continent has these tiny birds.

Some hummingbirds travel very far each year. The rufous hummingbird flies nearly 4,000 miles yearly.

These birds are amazing fliers. Some hummingbirds travel more than 500 miles over open ocean during migration without stopping once!

Hummingbirds remember every flower they visit and when it refills with nectar.

TEENY TINY

Hummingbirds live longer than many other birds. They can live up to 10 years in the wild!

Chirp! A bee hummingbird perches on a twig. It is barely bigger than a bumblebee.

Hummingbirds are the smallest birds on Earth. The bee hummingbird is the tiniest of all. It weighs less than a penny!

Most hummingbirds weigh about as much as a few paperclips. Their eggs are even smaller than jelly beans.

Despite their tiny size, hummingbirds are strong. They have powerful chest muscles for flying. Their tiny hearts work hard too, beating over 1,000 times per minute.

BRILLIANT BODIES

Flash! A ruby-throated hummingbird shows off its shiny red feathers.

Hummingbirds have special bodies built for flying. Their bones are hollow and light. This helps them move quickly through the air.

Their feathers shimmer in the sunlight. The colors change as they move. This happens because of how light bounces off them.

Hummingbirds have very long tongues. Their tongues split into two tips at the end. This shape helps them scoop nectar from deep inside of flowers.

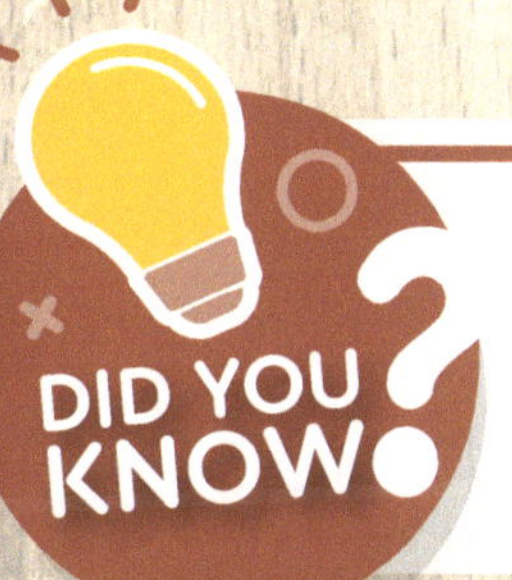

A hummingbird's brain can be about four percent of its body mass in some species!

SUPER
SIGHT

A hummingbird spots a flower far away. Its eyes see every detail.

Hummingbirds have amazing eyesight. They can see colors that humans cannot see, including ultraviolet light.

This makes flowers look different to hummingbirds. Special patterns on petals guide them to nectar. These patterns are invisible to people.

Hummingbirds can also see very fast movements. This helps them fly through tight spaces and spot danger quickly.

Hummingbirds can see nearly 360° in every direction at once!

STAY SAFE

Woosh! A hummingbird darts behind a leaf. It hides from danger.

Hummingbirds have many ways to stay safe. Their small size helps them hide in tight spots. They can squeeze between branches and leaves.

Some hummingbirds have dull colors on their backs. This helps them blend in with trees. Predators have trouble spotting them.

Hummingbirds are also very alert. They watch for danger while feeding. If scared, they can fly away in any direction instantly.

Some hummingbirds make alarm calls to warn other birds about predators nearby.

SWEET
SIPPERS

Sip! A hummingbird drinks from a bright orange flower.

Hummingbirds eat mostly **nectar** from flowers. Nectar is a sweet liquid that gives them the energy they need to fly.

These birds visit hundreds of flowers each day. They remember which flowers have the most nectar. They return to the best ones again and again.

Hummingbirds also eat tiny insects and spiders. These foods give them protein, which helps their muscles stay strong.

Nectar can be up to 50% sugar. It's like hummingbird candy!

HOVER AND SIP

Whirr! A hummingbird hangs in the air. It stays perfectly still.

Hummingbirds beat their wings up to 80 times per second. This super fast motion lets them **hover** in one spot. Their wings move so quickly that they make a humming sound. That is how these tiny birds got their name.

While hovering, hummingbirds drink nectar from flowers. Their long tongue works like a tiny pump. It traps the sweet liquid and pulls it into their mouth.

Without food, a hummingbird could starve in just a few hours. At night, they enter a deep sleep called "**torpor**" to save energy until morning.

WATCH OUT

DID YOU KNOW?
Roadrunners sometimes catch hummingbirds on the ground in deserts.

Screech! A hawk swoops down. A hummingbird zips away fast.

Hummingbirds face many dangers. Hawks, falcons, and other birds try to catch them. These **predators** are much bigger and have sharp talons.

Some snakes grab hummingbirds from branches. Large spiders can also trap them in webs. Even praying mantises can catch hummingbirds at flowers!

Cats are a danger too. Pet cats and wild cats hunt near feeders. This is why hummingbirds stay alert while feeding.

ZIP AWAY

Some hummingbirds dive at speeds over 45 miles per hour during courtship.

Swoosh! A hummingbird zips away through the branches. Another hummingbird is chasing it off!

Hummingbirds may be tiny, but they are fierce. They do not like to share. A hummingbird will guard its favorite flowers and chase away any bird that comes too close.

Remember, hummingbirds must eat constantly to survive. A patch of flowers can mean life or death. That is why they fight so hard to protect their food source.

Male hummingbirds are the most aggressive. They claim a territory and defend it all day long. They chase, dive-bomb, and even stab other hummingbirds with their sharp beaks.

FANTASTIC
FLIERS

Zoom! A hummingbird flies backward. It even spins in a circle!

Hummingbirds are amazing fliers. They can fly forward, backward, and sideways. They can even fly upside down for short moments.

Their wings rotate in a full circle. This special movement gives them total control. Few other birds can match these skills.

These tiny birds also travel far. Some **migrate** over 2,000 miles each year.

Hummingbirds flap their wings in a figure-eight pattern. This helps them stay balanced in the air.

BUSY BIRDS

DID YOU KNOW?

Hummingbirds digest a full meal of nectar in as little as 20 minutes — then they need to eat all over again!

Rustle! A hummingbird wakes at dawn and stretches its tiny wings.

A hummingbird's day starts with an emergency. After a long night in torpor, its body is low on energy. It must find food within minutes of waking up.

Once warmed up, the real work begins. A hummingbird may visit over 1,000 flowers in a single day. It zips from bloom to bloom, drinking nectar and chasing off rivals.

As the sun sets, the hummingbird finds a safe perch. Its heartbeat slows way down. Its body temperature drops. It enters torpor again, barely alive until morning.

FLYING
SOLO
28

Squeak! A hummingbird searches for flowers. Good! There are no other hummingbirds here.

Hummingbirds often live alone. They do not form flocks or families.

They like to find their own food sources. They do not share. Males and females only meet briefly to mate. Then they go off on their own again. Outside of mating season, a hummingbird has no flock, no partner, and no family group — just itself against the world.

Male hummingbirds do not help raise their babies at all. The mother does everything alone!

DAZZLING
DIVES

Thump! A male hummingbird dives from the sky. He zooms down fast!

Male hummingbirds perform dive displays. They fly high into the air and then zoom straight down at high speeds.

During the dive, their tail feathers make unique sounds. Different species make different sounds. Some tails chirp, while others whistle or pop.

Males repeat these dives many times. The displays show off their flying skills and bright colors.

Some male hummingbird tail feathers make sounds louder than a car horn during dives!

BITTY BABIES

Peep! A baby hummingbird opens its mouth wide. It is hungry!

Baby hummingbirds are called hatchlings. They hatch from eggs the size of a jellybean. Newborn chicks have no feathers and cannot see.

The mother feeds her babies by putting her beak into their mouths. She gives them tiny insects and nectar. Chicks eat many times each day.

All this food helps chicks grow fast. They get feathers in about two weeks. By three weeks old, most chicks are ready to fly and leave the nest.

MIGHTY MOMS

DID YOU KNOW?
A mother hummingbird builds her nest in about six to seven days, weaving it so tightly it can hold water!

Squawk! Tiny wings beat fast. A mom guards her babies.

Female hummingbirds raise their babies alone. Males do not help build nests or feed chicks. This means mothers do all the work.

The mother builds a tiny cup-shaped nest. She uses soft plant fluff and spider silk. This silk lets the nest stretch as babies grow bigger.

Mothers sit on their eggs to keep them warm. This takes about two weeks. Then she feeds chicks for three weeks until they can fly.

A mother may raise two sets of babies each year.

SURVIVORS

Zip! A hummingbird flies through a backyard looking for flowers.

Hummingbirds have lost many of their wild homes. Forests and meadows have been turned into cities and farms. But these tiny birds have found a way to survive, with help from people.

Many humans hang feeders filled with sugar water in their yards. Hummingbirds have learned that these red containers mean food. Some birds return to the same feeders year after year.

People also plant gardens with flowers that hummingbirds love. These backyard habitats have become important food stops, especially in cities where wild flowers are hard to find.

HUMMINGBIRD WATCHING

Swoosh! A hummingbird zips past a red flower.

People love to watch hummingbirds. These tiny birds visit gardens and parks. You can spot them near flowers.

Hummingbirds like certain plants. They visit trumpet-shaped blooms most often. Red and orange flowers attract them.

You can set up a feeder to watch them. Fill it with sugar water. Hang it in a shady spot. Then wait quietly nearby.

Some people hang dozens of feeders in their yards. They can attract hundreds of hummingbirds every day!

GLOSSARY

nectar

A sweet liquid inside flowers that hummingbirds drink for energy.

hover

To stay in one spot in the air without moving forward or backward.

torpor

A very deep sleep that helps hummingbirds save energy at night.

migrate

To travel a long way to a new home when the seasons change.

predators

Animals that hunt and eat other animals.